In the Beginning...

 S0-ADY-027

Consider This

A **prefix** is a group of letters added at the beginning of a word to change its meaning or to make a new word.

Prefix	Meaning	Word	Meaning
dis-	not	dislike	not like
dis-	reverse of	disappear	reverse of appear
il-	not	illegal	not legal
im-	not	impolite	not polite
re-	again	rewind	wind again
pre-	before	pretrial	before trial

Read each sentence. Choose the correct prefix to complete each underlined word.

1. The ▮game show starts 15 minutes before the game.

2. After being separated from the others, Mark and Ted gladly ▮joined the tour when they finally found them.

3. Because his alibi seemed far-fetched, the detective ▮believed the suspect's story.

4. The ▮literate man wished he could read the newspapers and books.

5. Since the huge rock was ▮movable, the Kelly family decided to plant their garden all around it.

6. The ▮obedient child refused to follow anyone's instructions.

7. My Uncle Fred ▮tells the same stories over and over.

8. Before takeoff, the mechanics give the airplane a ▮flight check.

9. The answer the witness gave was ▮logical; it made no sense at all.

10. Martina ▮agreed with Samuel because she thought his answer was wrong.

11. The high cost of your solution makes it ▮practical.

12. Harriet's desk was always in a state of ▮order; nothing was ever where it belonged.

C dis	H re	F pre
D re	J pre	L dis
A dis	C re	G il
H pre	E il	I re
G im	A re	B il
J re	I dis	D im
K re	D im	E pre
B im	L dis	J pre
F im	B il	K re
L dis	G il	A re
I pre	F dis	H im
E re	K pre	C dis

Objective: Identify correct prefixes, using context clues.

1

In the End ...

A **suffix** is a group of letters added to the end of a word to change its meaning or to make a new word.

Suffix	Meaning	Word	Meaning
-ful	full of	youthful	full of youth
-less	without	homeless	without a home
-ness	state of being	kindness	state of being kind
-ment	state of being	contentment	state of being content
-able	able to be	respectable	able to be respected

Read each sentence. Find the word that makes the best sense.

1 Amber was ▆ she had studied when she saw the test.

2 The kittens were so ▆, everyone stopped to look.

3 Zachary was ▆ because he was always willing to help his classmates.

4 Don't worry, it's just a garden snake—they're ▆.

5 Cheney spent several ▆ hours playing soccer.

6 Paco was sure he could make his car ▆ on time.

7 The portrait's ▆ to Adam was so true to life, I thought it might speak.

8 Raking leaves seemed like a tiresome and ▆ task.

9 The referee decided the ball was inbounds and still ▆.

10 Our check for classes was made ▆ to the school.

11 Standing in the sun without protection can be ▆ to your skin.

12 Sofia's ▆ of the ballet was shown by the smile on her face.

Answer Box

A	B	C	D	E	F
playful	payment	playable	likeable	thankful	harmless
G	**H**	**I**	**J**	**K**	**L**
thankless	enjoyment	harmful	enjoyable	payable	likeness

Objective: Identify correct suffixes in sentences.

Which Fix?

Choose the word that has a *prefix*.

1. disconnect   powerful
2. immoral   statement
3. lovable   prerecord
4. repay   manageable
5. fearless   illegal
6. discover   fitness

Remember, a prefix is added at the beginning of a word. A suffix is added at the end of a word.

Choose the word that has a *suffix*.

7. immoral   fitness
8. lovable   illegal
9. fearless   discover
10. prerecord   manageable
11. statement   disconnect
12. powerful   repay

Answer Box

A	B	C	D	E	F
statement	illegal	fitness	disconnect	lovable	powerful
G	**H**	**I**	**J**	**K**	**L**
fearless	prerecord	repay	manageable	immoral	discover

Objective: Discriminate between prefixes and suffixes.

3

The Root Is the Foundation

Consider This

A **root** is a word part that can be combined with prefixes, suffixes, and other roots to form new words.

-grat- pleasing or thankful   -hum- from the earth or ground
-scop- see   -phon- sound
-graph- written   -spec- look

Find the word that fits the definition.

1 full of thanks

2 something that is looked at for a specific reason

3 an involuntary response to a stimulus

4 a signature or, literally, self-written

5 one who is not thankful or pleasant

6 a device that transmits a written message at a distance

7 one who watches an event

8 a device that literally writes with sound; plays music

9 a device used to hear a sound or voice from far away

10 capable of being bent

11 a device used to see things that are a long way away

12 a device used to see things that are extremely small

Answer Box

A	B	C	D	E	F
phonograph	microscope	flexible	spectator	telescope	ingrate
G	**H**	**I**	**J**	**K**	**L**
specimen	telegraph	grateful	autograph	telephone	reflex

4   **Objective:** Match words with definitions, using word roots.

Compound Interest

Consider This

A **compound word** can be closed or open. If you put the word <u>cheese</u> between the words <u>cottage</u> ▮ <u>cake</u>, you make two compound words:

cottage cheese	**open compound word**
cheesecake	**closed compound word**

Make a word chain. Find the missing word to make two compound words.

A closed compound word is written as one word. An open compound word is written as two separate words.

1. police ▮ kind
2. cotton ▮ plant
3. side ▮ way
4. safety ▮ wheel
5. movie ▮ gaze
6. light ▮ lifter
7. every ▮ light
8. band ▮ still
9. stand ▮ life
10. tad ▮ star
11. note ▮ worm
12. book ▮ history

Answer Box

A	B	C	D	E	F
day	man	still	walk	weight	stand

G	H	I	J	K	L
pin	pole	book	star	case	seed

Objective: Form compound words by making word chains.

5

Alike or Opposite?

Find the *antonym* or *synonym* in the puzzle that matches each clue.

Across

1 synonym for compliment

6 synonym for build

7 antonym for hurt

8 antonym for generous

11 antonym for beautiful

12 antonym for fancy

Down

2 synonym for fancy

3 antonym for build

4 synonym for hurt

5 synonym for beautiful

9 antonym for compliment

10 synonym for generous

Remember, a synonym is a word that has the same or almost the same meaning as another word. An antonym is a word that has the opposite meaning of another word.

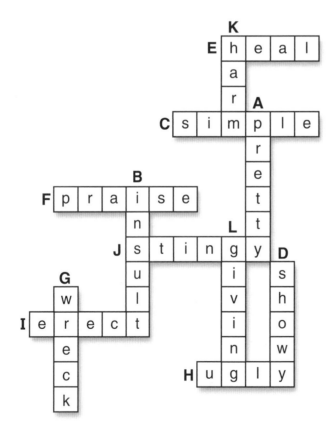

Objective: Identify words as synonyms or antonyms.

Shaping Your Vocabulary

Consider This

GEOMETRY TERMS

acute angle: angle measuring less than 90°

circumference: distance around a circle

diameter: distance across a circle through its center

equilateral triangle: triangle with three sides that have the same length

intersecting lines: lines that cross at one point

isosceles triangle: triangle with two sides that have the same length

obtuse angle: angle measuring more than 90°

parallel lines: lines in the same plane which do not cross or intersect

perpendicular lines: lines which cross at a right angle

radius: distance from the center of a circle to its edge

right triangle: triangle with one angle that measures 90°

scalene triangle: triangle with three sides that have different lengths

Use the definitions to help you determine the best name of each mathematical figure.

1

2

3

4

5

6

7

8

9

10

11

12

Answer Box

A	B	C	D	E	F
parallel lines	scalene triangle	obtuse angle	equilateral triangle	intersecting lines	acute angle
G	**H**	**I**	**J**	**K**	**L**
diameter	perpendicular lines	right triangle	circumference	radius	isosceles triangle

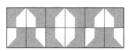

Objective: Match geometrical terms with drawings.

7

Look at Metric Measures

Choose the word in color that completes each sentence.

1 One (kilogram, kilometer) is equal to 0.6 of a mile.

2 One (decimeter, decameter) is equal to ten meters.

3 One (kiloliter, kilogram) is a measure of weight.

4 One (meter, liter) is a little longer than one yard.

5 One (kilogram, milligram) is smaller than one centigram.

6 One (decimeter, decameter) is less than a meter.

7 A (hectoliter, hectometer) is a good measurement for finding the distance between your house and your neighbor's house at the end of the block.

8 A (gram, meter) mass is often used with a balance scale.

9 One (centiliter, hectoliter) is less than one deciliter.

10 One hundred (centimeters, decimeters) equals one meter.

11 Ten (decaliters, kilometers) equals one hectoliter.

12 One (milliliter, hectoliter) is one thousandth of a liter.

The Metric System	
Prefix	Meaning
deca-	ten
hecto-	hundred
kilo-	thousand
deci-	tenth
centi-	hundredth
milli-	thousandth

meter: measurement of length
liter: measurement of volume
gram: measurement of weight

Answer Box

A	B	C	D	E	F
milliliter	decameter	kilogram	centiliter	hectometer	kilometer
G	H	I	J	K	L
decimeter	gram	decaliters	milligram	meter	centimeters

8 **Objective:** Identify metric measurement words, in context.

Eco-abulary

Read the article. Find the word that completes each sentence.

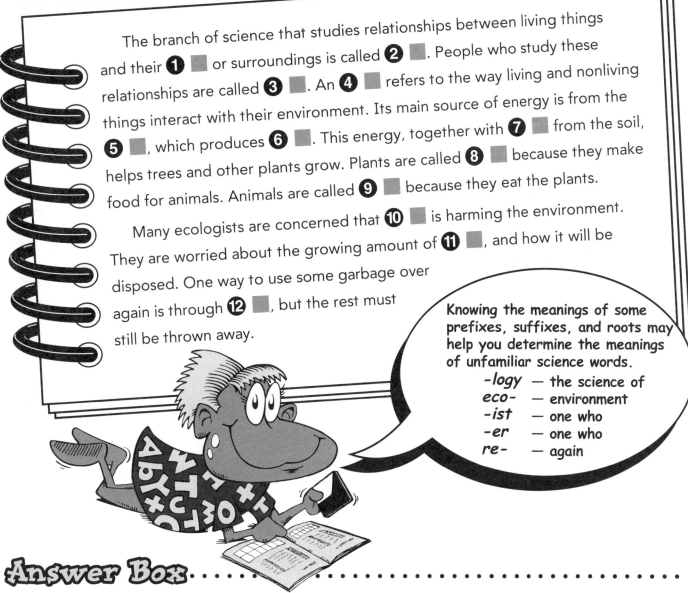

The branch of science that studies relationships between living things and their **1** ▢ or surroundings is called **2** ▢. People who study these relationships are called **3** ▢. An **4** ▢ refers to the way living and nonliving things interact with their environment. Its main source of energy is from the **5** ▢, which produces **6** ▢. This energy, together with **7** ▢ from the soil, helps trees and other plants grow. Plants are called **8** ▢ because they make food for animals. Animals are called **9** ▢ because they eat the plants.

Many ecologists are concerned that **10** ▢ is harming the environment. They are worried about the growing amount of **11** ▢, and how it will be disposed. One way to use some garbage over again is through **12** ▢, but the rest must still be thrown away.

Knowing the meanings of some prefixes, suffixes, and roots may help you determine the meanings of unfamiliar science words.

-logy	— the science of
eco-	— environment
-ist	— one who
-er	— one who
re-	— again

Answer Box

A	B	C	D	E	F
consumers	ecologists	nutrients	pollution	ecology	solar energy
G	H	I	J	K	L
sun	garbage	environment	ecosystem	recycling	producers

Objective: Discriminate between science words, in context.

9

Explosive Words

Match the definitions with the words in the diagram.

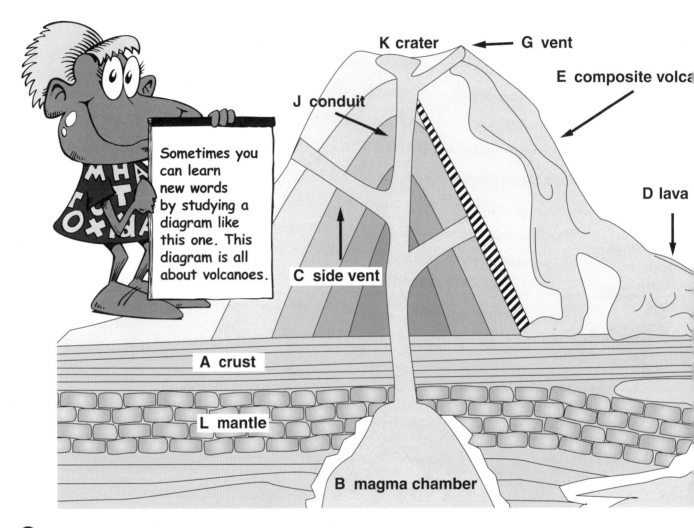

Sometimes you can learn new words by studying a diagram like this one. This diagram is all about volcanoes.

K crater

G vent

E composite volca[no]

J conduit

D lava

C side vent

A crust

L mantle

B magma chamber

❶ particles of pulverized rock blown out of a volcano during an eruption

❷ volcano formed over time from layers of cinder and ash that are released during a violent eruption

❸ volcano formed from layers of gently flowing lava and ash. These steep-sided, cone-shaped mountains can rise over 10,000 feet

❹ a passage formed as magma travels from the magma chamber to the opening of the volcano

❺ the round depression formed at the opening of the volcano

❻ the outer layer of the Earth's surface

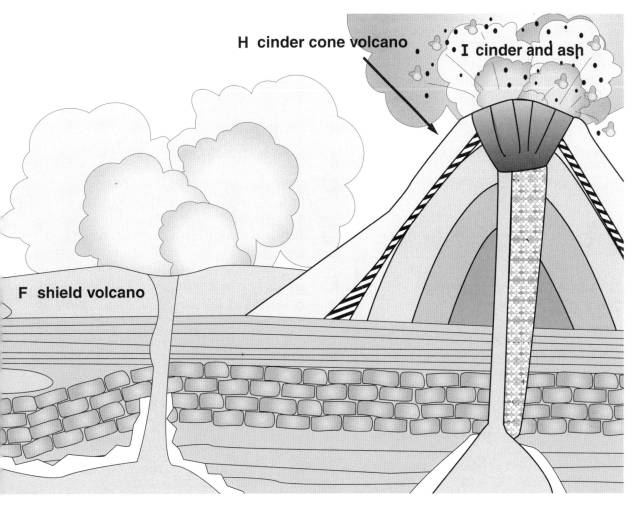

H cinder cone volcano

I cinder and ash

F shield volcano

7 liquid rock that flows in streams from the crater of a volcano during or following an eruption

8 cavity formed deep within the Earth that contains liquid magma

9 the layer of the Earth below its crust

10 openings in the side of the conduit which release some of the pressure caused by magma

11 a gently sloping volcano in the shape of a flattened dome

12 opening at the Earth's surface through which magma is released during an eruption

It's the American Way

Prefixes		Roots		Suffixes	
con-	together	-gress-	walk	-tion	act or result of
im-	not	-demo-	people	-ic	having the quality of
in-	not	-crat-	ruler, ruling body	-ment	result of
re-	again or back	-arch-	ruling body	-an	one believing in
de-	from, down	-mono-	one	-ant	a person who
ex-	out	-pend-	hang	-y	having the quality of
		-clar-	clear	-stit	form

Find the word that matches each definition. Use the chart to help you.

1 a government with one absolute ruler

2 a person who comes into a country to live there

3 something that is stated clearly and in public

4 the officials in charge of managing the affairs of a country or state and the results of their management

5 a body of rules that governs a community

6 to write over again, as in legislation

7 the lawmaking body of a republic; literally means "to walk together"

8 self-governing, freedom from control by others

9 the art of searching or traveling for the purpose of discovery, especially in a new country

10 a government that is run by the people living under it

11 a set of fundamental principles by which a nation is governed

12 coming into a country that is not one's own to settle there

Answer Box

A	B	C	D	E	F
government	democracy	declaration	constitution	redraw	independent
G	**H**	**I**	**J**	**K**	**L**
congress	monarchy	law	exploration	immigration	immigrant

Objective: Identify vocabulary words relating to social studies and U.S. history.

Money Talk

Find the word that best completes each sentence.

1 Selling something for more money than you paid for it creates a ■.

2 When people buy stock in a company, they are called ■ in the company.

3 Another word used for "products" produced by a company is ■.

4 Carpenters, gardeners, salespeople, and nurses are people who provide ■ for others.

5 To manage their money, people draw up a ■ that shows how their money should be spent.

6 When stores subtract a certain amount off the price of a product, they are selling the item for a ■.

7 Like blowing up a balloon, ■ refers to rising prices, salaries, and costs.

8 When people use a ■ card to buy something, they are actually borrowing money from the company that issues the card.

9 Someone who uses goods and services is called a ■.

10 Money that you receive from your salary at work or investments is ■.

11 If a company is spending more money than it earns, it is operating at a ■.

12 The price that is paid for something is also called its ■.

Answer Box

A	B	C	D	E	F
consumer	goods	investors	discount	services	profit
G	**H**	**I**	**J**	**K**	**L**
budget	loss	credit	cost	income	inflation

Objective: Identify vocabulary words that relate to social studies and economics, using context clues.

13

All Systems Go!

Consider This

Body systems are groups of organs that carry out major body activities. Here are descriptions of four of our body systems.

The **skeletal system** consists of bones that support the body and protect organs inside the body.

The **respiratory system** consists of those organs that help us breathe.

The **digestive system** consists of organs that help the body process and use food.

The **circulatory system** moves blood throughout the body.

Read each sentence. Choose the name of the system to which the word in color belongs.

1 The carpals are wrist bones.
  A circulatory system   H respiratory system   K skeletal system

2 The heart pumps blood by contracting and relaxing.
  G circulatory system   J skeletal system   L digestive system

3 When we inhale, air enters our body through the nose.
  D digestive system   I respiratory system   J circulatory system

4 The skull protects the brain.
  L skeletal system   B digestive system   D circulatory system

5 Air moves from the nose to the trachea, which is also called the windpipe.
  E circulatory system   C respiratory system   I skeletal system

6 The mouth is the first place where food is broken down.
  F skeletal system   K circulatory system   H digestive system

7 The arteries carry blood from the heart throughout the body.
  I digestive system   L skeletal system   E circulatory system

8 When we inhale, the chest expands as air fills the lungs.
  B respiratory system   A circulatory system   G skeletal system

9 In the stomach, acid and enzymes break down food.
  H skeletal system   D digestive system   C circulatory system

10 The veins carry blood to the heart.
  C digestive system   E skeletal system   F circulatory system

11 The small intestine completes the process of breaking down food.
  J digestive system   F circulatory system   B respiratory system

12 The sternum is also known as the breastbone.
  K respiratory system   G circulatory system   A skeletal system

Objective: Discriminate between vocabulary words relating to body systems.

Does It Compute?

Find the word and picture that matches the definition.

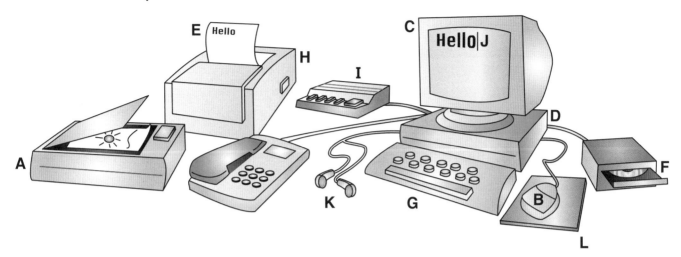

1 a piece of equipment that holds all the electronics necessary to process and store information

2 lets you listen privately to sound on the computer

3 hardware that prints out information from the computer

4 the computer screen where you view information you are working on

5 hardware used to move the cursor on the screen

6 an opening where you place a CD-ROM

7 a piece of hardware that connects your computer to a phone line

8 a printed version of the information on the computer screen

9 a piece of hardware that allows you to scan information from loose sheets of paper into your computer

10 an arrow that shows you where you will type next on the screen

11 the board that holds the keys used for entering information

12 the pad underneath the mouse

Answer Box

A	B	C	D	E	F
scanner	mouse	monitor	computer	hardcopy	CD-ROM drive
G	**H**	**I**	**J**	**K**	**L**
keyboard	printer	modem	cursor	headphones	mouse pad

Objective: Identify computer content vocabulary. 15

Bon Appetit!

Read the menu with food names from around the world.
Find the origin of each food named below.

International Cuisine

_ _ _ _ _ _ _ _ _ _ _ _ _ _ _

Breakfast
1 waffles with **2** syrup (sweet liquid)

3 bagel

Lunch or Dinner
4 noodles with butter

5 spaghetti with sauce

6 chili with cheese

7 broccoli with **8** croutons

Desserts
9 cookie

10 pretzel

Beverages
11 cider

12 hot chocolate

Answer Box

A	B	C	D	E	F
brezel (Germany)	nudeln (Germany)	koekje (Netherlands)	spago (Italy)	croûte (France)	chili con queso (Mexico)

G	H	I	J	K	L
wafel (Netherlands)	broccolo (Italy)	sidre (England)	beygl (Israel)	šarāb (Arabia)	xocolatl (Mexico)

Objective: Recognize words from other languages with similar qualities to English words.

Where in the World?

Match the words with their country of origin.

1. hors d'oeuvre
2. squash
3. kindergarten
4. graffiti
5. karate
6. alligator

Many words in our language are borrowed from other countries. A good dictionary will give you the history, or etymology, of many words. Often it is in brackets.

Match each word with its meaning.

7. eureka
8. veranda
9. status quo
10. cul-de-sac
11. fiasco
12. khaki

Answer Box

A	B	C	D	E	F
as usual	Germany	United States	Spain	Italy	France
G	**H**	**I**	**J**	**K**	**L**
Japan	a failure	porch with a roof	yellowish brown	dead end	"I found it!"

Objective: Identify origin for words borrowed from other languages. Match meanings to borrowed words.

17

It's Greek to Me

> Use the Greek roots to help you build the meanings of the words!

Consider This

Greek Roots

-hydr-	water		-geo-	earth
-astro-	star		-graph-	write
-bio-	life		-naut-	ship or sailor
			-nom-	order

Find the word that fits the definition.

1 the study of the history of the earth

2 a large upright pipe from which water can be drawn for fighting fires

3 having the quality of writing or drawing

4 keeping oneself in order; independence

5 one who studies the order of stars

6 one who travels among the stars

7 self-written account of one's own life

8 to lose, or cause to lose, water or moisture

9 the study of physical, biological, and cultural features of the earth's surface

10 having to do with ships, sailors, navigators

11 the study of stars

12 the study of life

Answer Box

A	B	C	D	E	F
nautical	autobiography	astronaut	hydrant	astronomy	astronomer
G	**H**	**I**	**J**	**K**	**L**
autonomy	geology	biology	dehydrate	graphic	geography

18   **Objective:** Match words with Greek roots to their literal definitions.

Play It Safe!

Find the place where each direction would most likely be found.

1 Use before April 10th

2 Danger: falling rocks

3 Keep out of reach of children

4 No diving

5 Danger: thin ice

6 Danger: polluted area

Match each direction with its meaning.

7 Wear protective eye gear

8 Do not inhale fumes

9 Take only as directed

10 Keep out

11 Caution: flammable

12 Caution: may cause drowsiness

Answer Box

A	B	C	D	E	F
Follow doctor's instructions when taking this drug.	medicine bottle	Be careful; using this drug could make you sleepy.	Do not breathe in the odors.	container of milk	swimming pool

G	H	I	J	K	L
skating pond	Be careful; contents could catch fire.	dumping ground	beside a cliff	Use safety goggles to shield your eyes.	Do not enter this area.

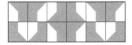

Let the Buyer Beware!

Match the common consumer phrase with its meaning.

1 Once you buy an item, you cannot get your money back.

2 You must show an identification card, such as a driver's license, to show proof of your age.

3 Credit cards and checks are not accepted.

4 The item you purchased will be brought to your home without cost to you.

5 Food service available without leaving your car.

6 Pump gasoline yourself.

7 No change will be given.

8 Identifies the place where you must pay for your purchase.

9 A device that enables you to deposit or withdraw money at your bank.

10 No one under the age of 21 can enter a particular place or buy a particular product.

11 Line in a grocery store for people with only a few items.

12 You can take 30 days to pay without being charged interest.

Signs and notices with important information are all around us. Where have you seen these phrases before?

Answer Box

A	B	C	D	E	F
self-service pumps	ID required	drive-up window	10 items or less	no refunds	free delivery
G	**H**	**I**	**J**	**K**	**L**
pay here	30 days same as cash	automated teller machine (ATM)	cash only	exact change only	must be 21

Objective: Identify and use consumer information phrases.

On the Job

Find the word that matches each definition.

1 person who hires others

2 person who can tell someone else about your character or your ability to do the job

3 booklet that provides the employee with information about the job and job-related procedures

4 extras beyond salary given to the employee

5 fixed payment given to the employee for regular work

6 form person fills out before being hired in order to give the employer information about himself or herself

7 a brief written description of one's experience and education

8 money taken out of your salary which is paid to the government

9 person who works for another

10 a person who oversees other people at work

11 a card that shows the numbers of hours that an employee has worked

12 a person's name, written by that person

Every area of life has its own set of special words. Use the dictionary to help you learn any unfamiliar words.

Answer Box

A	B	C	D	E	F
manual	employee	manager	résumé	reference	application

G	H	I	J	K	L
time card	salary	benefits	employer	signature	taxes

Objective: Identify and use work-related phrases.

21

Watch for Signs

Find the meaning of each sign.

1

2

3

ENTRANCE

4

DETOUR

5

6

7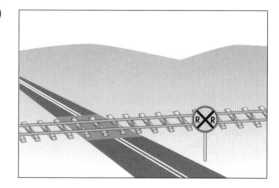

EXIT

8

FIRE EXIT

9

10

11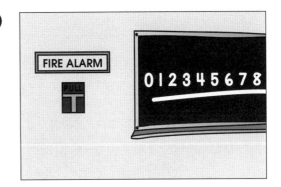

FIRE ALARM
PULL

0 1 2 3 4 5 6 7 8

12

HAZARDOUS AREA

Answer Box

A	B	C	D	E	F
bicycle crossing	railroad crossing	women's restroom	exit through this door	enter through this door	stairs are located through the door
G	**H**	**I**	**J**	**K**	**L**
this area is dangerous; use caution	use this exit in case there is a fire	men's restroom	you must take an alternate route	In case of fire, pull the switch for the fire alarm.	wheelchair access

Objective: Recognize informational signs and match them with their meanings.

City Sights

Find the phrase that tells what you would do at each place.

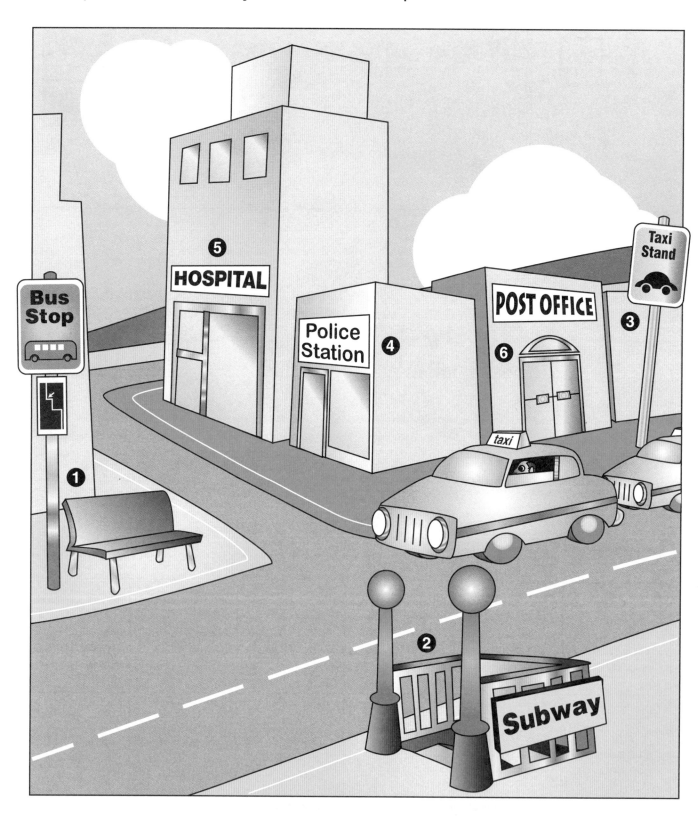

Find the place name that matches each description.

7 an emergency exit used in case of fire

8 an apparatus used to go from one floor to another

9 a place to board a bus for a long trip or to meet someone who is arriving on a bus

10 a place to catch a train or to meet someone who is arriving on a train

11 underground transportation

12 a place where heavy construction is being done

Answer Box

A	B	C	D	E	F
subway	catch a taxi cab	enter the subway	mail a letter	catch a bus	fire escape
G	**H**	**I**	**J**	**K**	**L**
bus station	get an injury treated	hard hat area	elevator	train station	report a crime

Objective: Use the pictures and definitions to identify place names and functions.

25

Let's Talk Turkey

Consider This

An **idiom** is a group of words that means something different from what the words actually say. "John is all thumbs" doesn't mean that John has all thumbs and no fingers. It means John is clumsy.

Match each idiom shown in color with its meaning.

1. When we presented our idea, the teacher gave us the green light to begin.

2. The car was a real lemon; it was always in the shop.

3. Mr. Roberts is often asked to give speeches and toasts; he has a silver tongue.

4. Ms. Wilson makes all the decisions; she is the top banana in the office.

5. The three students who won scholarships were the cream of the crop in our school.

6. Jed would not get the project done in time; he was up a creek without a paddle.

7. Yorktown rolled out the red carpet for the visiting rock star.

8. We thought our proposal was strong, but our boss showed us the red light.

9. I don't have a chance of winning a tennis match against Fiona; she is out of my league.

10. Paul decided to close his restaurant forever; the fire was the last straw.

11. The fiftieth anniversary party was a golden moment for Larry and Jean.

12. Rodney ripped up his speech; he decided to wing it instead.

Answer Box

A	B	C	D	E	F
in a hopeless situation	a bad product	at a different skill level	the best	most important person	gave permission

G	H	I	J	K	L
do something without preparing ahead	disapproved; told us to stop	a special time	is a good speaker	gave special treatment	final event that causes someone to make a decision

Objective: Match idioms with meanings, using context clues.

I'm All Ears

Look at each picture. Determine the idiom that it represents and its meaning.

1 idiom
2 meaning

7 idiom
8 meaning

3 idiom
4 meaning

9 idiom
10 meaning

5 idiom
6 meaning

11 idiom
12 meaning

Answer Box

A	B	C	D	E	F
My dad told me to quit beating around the bush.	My brother always puts his foot in his mouth.	was hoarse	In my family, Dad brings home the bacon.	earns money	told something she shouldn't have

G	H	I	J	K	L
My aunt spilled the beans.	My mother had a frog in her throat.	My mother told me to shake a leg.	not getting to the point	hurry up	says dumb things

Objective: Match illustrations with idioms and their meanings.

Find the Connection

Consider This

Analogies show a likeness in some way between things that are otherwise unlike. In this analogy, the relationship between a <u>car</u> and a <u>garage</u> is similar to the relationship between a <u>horse</u> and a <u>stable</u>.

<u>Car</u> is to <u>garage</u> as <u>horse</u> is to <u>stable</u> is an analogy.

Find the word that completes each analogy.

1. Comedian is to joke as singer is to ■.
2. Bird is to sky as fish is to ■.
3. Night is to moon as day is to ■.
4. Movie is to watch as book is to ■.
5. Sun is to star as Mars is to ■.
6. Mouse is to cheese as monkey is to ■.
7. Ant is to hill as bird is to ■.
8. Keyboard is to hand as pedal is to ■.
9. Yellow is to banana as red is to ■.
10. Smell is to nose as see is to ■.
11. Writer is to book as sculptor is to ■.
12. Beagle is to dog as robin is to ■.

Answer Box

A	B	C	D	E	F
foot	bird	nest	eye	statue	planet
G	**H**	**I**	**J**	**K**	**L**
sea	banana	read	song	apple	sun

28

Objective: Recognize the relationships to complete analogies.

___ Is to ___ As ___ Is to ___

Find the word that completes each analogy.

1 Foot is to toe as hand is to ■.

2 Bag is to plastic as log is to ■.

3 Police officer is to law as referee is to ■.

4 Fire is to water as dirt is to ■.

5 Wood is to fire as fuel is to ■.

6 Doctor is to hospital as waiter is to ■.

7 Two is to twins as three is to ■.

8 Plate is to sandwich as bowl is to ■.

9 Court is to tennis as field is to ■.

10 Three is to triangle as four is to ■.

11 Foot is to leg as hand is to ■.

12 Teacher is to school as judge is to ■.

Think about how the first pair of words goes together. Then find the word that makes the second pair of words go together in the same way.

Answer Box

A	B	C	D	E	F
finger	soap	car	arm	wood	restaurant

G	H	I	J	K	L
square	triplets	baseball	rules	soup	court

Objective: Recognize relationships to complete analogies.

29

Riddle Me This!

Find the word or phrase that solves each riddle.

1 What kind of a song would you sing while driving?

2 What do you call a singing sea creature?

3 What do you feel when you take off your socks?

4 What did the tourists take on their sightseeing trip?

5 What kind of tree barks?

6 What kind of tree smells sweet?

7 What did the father call his boy who was born under water?

8 What did the father call his boy who was born in a tree?

9 What do you call a hot drink that is made from wood?

10 What did the old man do when his bicycle punctured a tube?

11 How do you describe a group of campers asleep at night?

12 What is a young doctor who gets called back as he is going out the door?

A riddle poses a puzzling question, statement, or problem.

Answer Box

A	B	C	D	E	F
a cartoon	a detour	an intern	a tuna fish	treaty	defeat

G	H	I	J	K	L
retired	season	a rosewood	treason	intense	a dogwood

30   **Objective:** Solve riddles involving word play.

It's a Pig's Life

Find the answer to each riddle.

1 What does a pig wear around its neck for good luck?

2 What kind of pig works in an embassy?

3 What do you use to take a pig to a hospital?

4 What does a pig use to clean a bathroom?

5 What do you call a pig that lives in the United States?

6 What word would you use to describe a pig that wants to succeed?

7 What do you call it when a pig loses his memory?

8 What does a pig in a rock band use?

9 What is a pig's favorite flower?

10 What do you call a pig that plays sports, but is not a professional?

11 What do you call a group of pigs that play music?

12 What word would you use to describe a pig that does unbelievable things?

Don't be afraid to ham it up on this activity.

Answer Box

A	B	C	D	E	F
a hamerican	a porkestra	hamazing	a hamplifier	a hamateur	hamnesia
G	**H**	**I**	**J**	**K**	**L**
a porkid	a hambulance	hambitious	a hambassador	hammonia	a hamulet

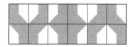

Objective: Solve riddles involving word play.   31

Tom Swifties

Consider This

To create a **Tom Swifty**, use two related words in an interesting, unexpected, or funny way.

"Let's <u>hurry</u>," said Ned <u>swiftly</u>.

Find the word that completes each sentence.

1. "Your sewing is extremely sloppy," her mother ▨.

2. "The temperature is dropping," said Pamela ▨.

3. "The hen just laid an egg," ▨ the farmer's daughter.

4. "Don't use that knife!" said Mother ▨.

5. The clumsy woodcutter ▨ through the woods looking for a tree to cut down.

6. "My rooster is the best alarm clock around," Selma ▨.

7. "That's not much of a fish," Edwin ▨.

8. Walter ▨ for a tree that was in the window of the plant store.

9. "Stay back! It's a bomb!" the police officer ▨.

10. "I love the shine of a polished floor," said Marina ▨.

11. "My throat is parched. I need a drink," said Sid ▨.

12. "That is one big fish!" Andrew ▨.

Answer Box

A	B	C	D	E	F
crowed	pined	boomed	cackled	carped	needled
G	**H**	**I**	**J**	**K**	**L**
wailed	coldly	lumbered	dryly	sharply	brightly

Objective: Practice word play by completing Tom Swifties.